To

From

A

DON'T SWEAT
THE SMALL STUFF

Treasury

Also by the Author

Don't Sweat the Small Stuff in Love
Don't Sweat the Small Stuff at Work
Don't Sweat the Small Stuff with Your Family
Don't Worry, Make Money
Don't Sweat the Small Stuff . . . And It's All Small Stuff
Slowing Down to the Speed of Life (with Joseph Bailey)
Handbook for the Heart (with Benjamin Shield)
Handbook for the Soul (with Benjamin Shield)
Shortcut Through Therapy
You Can Feel Good Again
You Can Be Happy No Matter What

Don't Sweat the Small Stuff Treasuries:

A Special Selection for Fathers
A Special Selection for Mothers
A Special Selection for Graduates
A Special Selection for Teachers
A Special Collection for Newlyweds
A Special Collection for Friends
A Special Collection for the Office

A DON'T SWEAT THE SMALL STUFF *Treasury*

A Special Collection for New Parents

Richard Carlson, Ph.D.

A Don't Sweat the Small Stuff Treasury
A Special Collection for New Parents

Copyright © 2000, Richard Carlson, Ph.D.

ISBN: 0-7868-6626-8

Library of Congress Catalog Card Number: 99-37512

FIRST EDITION
10 9 8 7 6 5 4 3 2 1

Contents

Introduction

Congratulations on becoming a new parent! I'm extremely happy for you as you embark on the incredible journey of parenthood. To me, there is no more important, or potentially joyful, experience in life.

There's no question that two of the happiest days of my life were the days my two daughters were born. The joy I felt was, and still is, indescribable. As a new parent, you either already have had, or are about to experience, a similar feeling. Most parents will tell you there's nothing quite like it. The love you feel is like none other.

It's strange that something so magical and

wonderful could also be so stressful! But the truth is, between all the new responsibilities, not knowing what to expect, sleep deprivation, and everything else associated with being a new parent, the experience often is just that—stressful! Again, this doesn't detract from the joy and wonder of it all—but it is hard work, and it can be a little overwhelming.

Being a parent myself, I've put a great deal of time into reflecting on ways to be the best, happiest, and calmest parent I can be. I know that as a parent, there are many important decisions regarding "big stuff" that must be made on a regular basis and, as our children grow up, there are many critical things to attend to. Often, our choices regarding our children are of monumental importance to their future, and these choices aren't always easy to make. To me, that's precisely why it's so important that we learn not to sweat the small stuff; there are simply too many more important things to take care of and think about.

It's for that reason that I created this little book especially for new parents. I've carefully selected strategies from my *Don't Sweat* books that seem to be most useful in helping new parents become less stressed, happier people. The strategies you are about to read are the ones that new parents have told me have been the most helpful to them, and the ones that helped me the most when I was a new parent. They are designed to heighten your perspective and gratitude, nurture your relationship with your child and with yourself, and to help you remain relaxed, calm, and happy.

If you are a new parent, I salute you and thank you. You have taken on the world's most important job—parenting. Thank you for doing your best to bring up a wonderful, happy child. I hope this little book serves you well.

Treasure the gift of children,

Richard Carlson

Don't Sweat the Small Stuff

Often we allow ourselves to get all worked up about things that, upon closer examination, *aren't* really that big a deal. We focus on little problems and concerns and blow them way out of proportion. A stranger, for example, might cut in front of us in traffic. Rather than let it go, and go on with our day, we convince ourselves that we are justified in our anger. Many of us might even tell someone else about the incident later on rather than simply let it go.

Why not instead simply allow the driver to have his accident somewhere else? Try to have compassion for the person and remember how painful it is to be in such an enormous hurry. This way, we can maintain our own sense of well-being and avoid taking other people's problems personally.

There are many similar, "small stuff" examples that occur every day in our lives. Whether we had to wait in line, listen to unfair criticism, or do the lion's share of the work, it pays enormous dividends if we learn not to worry about little things. So many people spend so much of their life energy "sweating the small stuff" that they completely lose touch with the magic and beauty of life. When you commit to working toward this goal you will find that you will have far more energy to be kinder and gentler.

2.

Make Peace with Imperfection

I've yet to meet an absolute perfectionist whose life was filled with inner peace. The need for perfection and the desire for inner tranquility conflict with each other. Whenever we are attached to having something a certain way, better than it already is, we are, almost by definition, engaged in a losing battle. Rather than being content and grateful for what we have, we are focused on what's wrong with something and our need to fix it. We are zeroed in on what's wrong, it implies that we are dissatisfied, discontent.

Whether it's related to ourselves—a disorganized

closet, a scratch on the car, an imperfect accomplishment, a few pounds we would like to lose—or someone else's imperfections—the way someone looks, behaves, or lives their life—the very act of focusing on imperfection pulls us away from our goal of being kind and gentle. This strategy has nothing to do with ceasing to do your very best but with being overly attached and focused on what's wrong with life. It's about realizing that while there's always a better way to do something, this doesn't mean that you can't enjoy and appreciate the way things already are.

The solution here is to catch yourself when you fall into your habit of insisting that things should be other than they are. Gently remind yourself that life is okay the way it is, right now. In the absence of your judgment, everything would be fine. As you begin to eliminate your need for perfection in all areas of your life, you'll begin to discover the perfection in life itself.

3

Learn to Live in the Present Moment

To a large degree, the measure of our peace of mind is determined by how much we are able to live in the present moment. Irrespective of what happened yesterday or last year, and what may or may not happen tomorrow, the present moment is where you are—always!

Without question, many of us have mastered the neurotic art of spending much of our lives worrying about a variety of things—all at once. We allow past problems and future concerns to dominate our present moments, so much so we end up anxious, frustrated, depressed, and hopeless. On the flip side, we also postpone our gratification, our stated priorities, and our happiness, often convincing ourselves that "someday" will be better than today. Unfortunately, the same mental dynamics that tell us to look toward the future will only repeat themselves so that "someday" never actually arrives. John Lennon once said, "Life is what's happening while we're busy making other plans." When we're busy making "other plans," our children are busy growing up, the people we love are moving away and dying, our bodies are getting out of shape, and our dreams are slipping away. In short, we miss out on life.

Many people live as if life were a dress rehearsal for some later date. It isn't. In fact, no one has a guarantee that he or she will be here tomorrow. Now is the only time we have, and the only time that we have any control over. When our attention is in the present moment, we push fear from our minds. Fear is the concern over events that might happen in the future—we won't have enough money, our children will get into trouble, we will get old and die, whatever.

To combat fear, the best strategy is to learn to bring your attention back to the present. Mark Twain said, "I have been through some terrible things in my life, some of which actually happened." I don't think I can say it any better. Practice keeping your attention on the here and now. Your efforts will pay great dividends.

4

Create "Practice Patience Periods"

Patience is a quality of heart that can be greatly enhanced with deliberate practice. An effective way that I have found to deepen my own patience is to create actual practice periods—periods of time that I set up in my mind to practice the art of patience. Life itself becomes a classroom, and the curriculum is patience.

You can start with as little as five minutes and build up your capacity for patience, over time. Start by saying to yourself, "Okay, for the next five minutes I won't allow myself to be bothered by anything. I'll be patient." What you'll discover is truly amazing. Your intention to be patient, especially if you know it's only for a short while, immediately strengthens your capacity for patience. Patience is one of those special qualities where success feeds on itself. Once you reach little milestones—five minutes of successful patience—you'll begin to see that you do, indeed, have the capacity to be patient, even for longer periods of time. Over time, you may even become a patient person.

Since I have young children at home, I have many possibilities to practice the art of patience. For example, on a day when both girls are firing questions at me as I'm trying to make important phone calls, I'll say to myself, "Now is a great time to be patient. For the next half hour I'm going to try to be as patient as possible (see, I've worked hard, I'm up to thirty minutes)!" All kidding aside, it really works—and it has worked in our family. As I keep my cool and don't allow myself to be annoyed and upset, I can calmly, yet firmly, direct my children's behavior far more effectively than when I get crazy. The simple act of gearing my mind toward patience allows me to remain in the present moment far more than when I would if I were upset, thinking about all the times this has happened before and feeling like a martyr. What's more, my patient feelings are often contagious—they rub off on the kids, who then decide, on their own, that it's no fun to bother Dad.

Being patient allows me to keep my perspective. I can remember, even in the midst of a difficult situation, that what's before me—my present challenge—isn't "life or death" but simply a minor obstacle that must be dealt with. Without patience, the same scenario can become a major emergency complete with yelling, frustration, hurt feelings, and high blood pressure. It's really not worth all that. Whether you're needing to deal with children, your boss, or a difficult person or situation—if you don't want to "sweat the small stuff," improving your patience level is a great way to start.

5.

Ask Yourself the Question, "Will This Matter a Year from Now?"

Almost every day I play a game with myself that I call "time warp." I made it up in response to my consistent, erroneous belief that what I was all worked up about was really important.

To play "time warp," all you have to do is imagine that whatever circumstances you are dealing with aren't happening right now but a year from now. Then simply ask yourself, "Is this situation really as important as I'm making it out to be?" Once in a great while it may be—but a vast majority of the time, it simply isn't.

Whether it be an argument with your spouse, child, or boss, a mistake, a lost opportunity, a lost wallet, a work-related rejection, or a sprained ankle, chances are, a year from now you aren't going to care. It will be one more irrelevant detail in your life. While this simple game won't solve all your problems, it can give you an enormous amount of needed perspective. I find myself laughing at things I used to take far too seriously. Now, rather than using up my energy feeling angry and overwhelmed, I can use it instead on spending time with my wife and children or engaging in creative thinking.

6.

Set Aside Quiet Time, Every Day

As I begin to write this strategy, it's exactly 4:30 in the morning, my favorite time of the day. I still have at least an hour and a half before my wife and children get out of bed and the phone begins to ring; at least an hour before anyone can ask me to do anything. It's absolutely silent outside and I'm in complete solitude. There is something rejuvenating and peaceful about being alone and having some time to reflect, work, or simply enjoy the quiet.

I've been working in the stress management field for well over a decade. In that time I've met some extraordinary people. I can't think of a single person whom I would consider to be inwardly peaceful who doesn't carve out at least a little quiet time, virtually every day. Whether it's ten minutes of meditation or yoga, spending a little time in nature, or locking the bathroom door and taking a ten-minute bath, quiet time to yourself is a vital part of life. Like spending time alone, it helps to balance the noise and confusion that infiltrate much of our day. Personally, when I set aside quiet time for myself, it makes the rest of my day seem manageable. When I don't, I really notice the difference.

There's a little ritual that I do that I've shared with many friends. Like many people, I drive to and from my office on a daily basis. On my way home from work, as I get close to my driveway, I pull my car over and stop. There is a nice spot where I can spend a minute or two looking at the view or closing my eyes and breathing. It slows me down and helps me feel centered and grateful. I've shared this strategy with dozens of people who used to complain about having "no time for quiet." They would speed into their driveways with the radio blaring in their ears. Now, with a simple shift in their actions, they enter their homes feeling much more relaxed.

7.

Imagine the People in Your Life as Tiny Infants and as One-Hundred-Year-Old Adults

I learned this technique almost twenty years ago. It has proven to be extremely successful for releasing feelings of irritation toward other people.

Think of someone who truly irritates you, who makes you feel angry. Now, close your eyes and try to imagine this person as a tiny infant. See their tiny little features and their innocent little eyes. Know that babies can't help but make mistakes and each of us was, at one time, a little infant. Now, roll forward the clock one hundred years. See the same person as a very old person who is about to die. Look at their worn-out eyes and their soft smile, which suggests a bit of wisdom and the admission of mistakes made. Know that each of us will be one hundred years old, alive or dead, before too many decades go by.

You can play with this technique and alter it in many ways. It almost always provides the user with some needed perspective and compassion. If our goal is to become more peaceful and loving, we certainly don't want to harbor negativity toward others.

8

See the Glass as Already Broken (and Everything Else Too)

This is a Buddhist teaching that I learned over twenty years ago. It has provided me, again and again, with greatly needed perspective to guide me toward my goal of a more accepting self.

The essence of this teaching is that all life is in a constant state of change. Everything has a beginning and everything has an end. Every tree begins with a seed and will eventually transform back into the earth. Every rock is formed and every rock will vanish. In our modern world, this means that every car, every machine, every piece of clothing is created and will all wear out and crumble; it's only a matter of when. Our bodies are born and they will die. A glass is created and will eventually break.

There is peace to be found in this teaching. When you expect something to break, you're not surprised or disappointed when it does. Instead of becoming immobilized when something is destroyed, you feel grateful for the time you have had.

The easiest place to start is with simple things, a glass of water, for example. Pull out your favorite drinking glass. Take a moment to look at and appreciate its beauty and all it does for you. Now, imagine that same glass as already broken, shattered all over the floor. Try to maintain the perspective that, in time, everything disintegrates and returns to its initial form.

Obviously, no one wants their favorite drinking glass, or anything else, to be broken. This philosophy is not a prescription for becoming passive or apathetic, but for making peace with the way things are. When your drinking glass does break, this philosophy allows you to maintain perspective. Rather than thinking, "Oh my God," you'll find yourself thinking, "Ah, there it goes." Play with this awareness and you'll find yourself not only keeping your cool but appreciating life as never before.

9.

Do One Thing at a Time

The other day I was driving on the freeway and noticed a man who, while driving in the fast lane, was shaving, drinking a cup of coffee, and reading the newspaper! "Perfect," I thought to myself, as just that morning I was trying to think of an appropriate example to point out the craziness of our frenzied society.

How often do we try to do more than one thing at once? We have cordless phones that are supposed to make our lives easier, but in some respects, they make our lives more confusing. My wife and I were at a friend's home for dinner a while ago and noticed her talking on the phone while simultaneously answering the door, checking on dinner, and changing her daughter's diaper (after she washed her hands, of course)! Many of us have the same tendency when we're speaking to someone and our mind is somewhere else, or when we're doing three or four chores all at the same time.

When you do too many things at once, it's impossible to be present-moment oriented. Thus, you may not only lose out on much of the potential enjoyment of what you are doing, but you also become far less focused and effective.

An interesting exercise is to block periods of time where you commit to doing only one thing at a time. Whether you're washing dishes, talking on the phone, driving a car, playing with your child, talking to your spouse, or reading a magazine, try to focus only on that one thing. Be present in what you are doing. Concentrate. You'll notice two things beginning to happen. First, you'll actually enjoy what you are doing, even something mundane like washing dishes or cleaning out a closet. When you're focused, rather than distracted, it enables you to become absorbed and interested in your activity, whatever it might be. Second, you'll be amazed at how quickly and efficiently you'll get things done. Since I've become more present-moment oriented, my skills have increased in virtually all areas of my life—writing, reading, cleaning house, and speaking on the phone. You can do the same thing. It all starts with your decision to do one thing at a time.

Practice Being in the "Eye of the Storm"

The eye of the storm is that one specific spot in the center of a twister, hurricane, or tornado that is calm, almost isolated from the frenzy of activity. Everything around the center is violent and turbulent, but the center remains peaceful. How nice it would be if we too could be calm and serene in the midst of chaos—in the eye of the storm.

Surprisingly enough, it's much easier than you might imagine to be in the eye of a "human storm." What it takes is intention and practice. Suppose, for example, that you are going to a family gathering that is going to be chaotic. You can tell yourself that you are going to use the experience as an opportunity to remain calm. You can commit to being the one person in the room who is going to be an example of peace. You can practice breathing. You can practice listening. You can let others be right and enjoy the glory. The point is, you can do it if you set your mind to it.

By starting out with harmless scenarios like family gatherings, cocktail parties, and birthday parties for children, you can build a track record and enjoy some success. You'll notice that by being in the eye of the storm, you will be more present-moment oriented. You'll enjoy yourself more than ever before. Once you have mastered harmless circumstances like these, you can practice on more difficult areas of life—dealing with conflict, hardship, or grief. If you start slowly, have some success, and keep practicing, pretty soon you'll know how to live in the eye of the storm.

Be Flexible with Changes in Your Plans

Once I get something in my mind (a plan), it can be tricky to let go of it and go with the flow. I was taught, and to some degree it's certainly true, that success, or successfully completing a project, requires perseverance. At the same time, however, inflexibility creates an enormous amount of inner stress and is often irritating and insensitive to other people.

I like to do the majority of my writing in the wee hours of the morning. I might have the goal, in this book for example, to complete one or two strategies before anyone else in the house wakes up. But what happens if my four-year-old wakes up early and walks upstairs to see me? My plans have certainly been altered, but how do I react? Or, I might have the goal to go out for a run before going to the office. What happens if I get an emergency call from the office and have to skip my run?

There are countless potential examples for all of us—times when our plans suddenly change, something we thought was going to take place doesn't, someone doesn't do what they said they would do, you make less money than what you thought you would, someone changes your plans without your consent, you have less time than previously planned, something unexpected comes up—and on and on it goes. The question to ask yourself is, What's *really* important?

We often use the excuse that it's natural to be frustrated when our plans change. That depends, however, on what your priorities are. Is it more important to stick to some rigid writing schedule or to be available to my four-year-old? Is missing a thirty-minute run worth getting upset over? The more general question is, "What's more important, getting what I want and keeping my plans, or learning to go with the flow?" Clearly, to become a more peaceful person, you must prioritize being flexible over rigidity most of the time (obviously there will be exceptions). I've also found it helpful to *expect* that a certain percentage of plans will change. If I make allowances in my mind for this inevitability, then when it happens I can say, "Here is one of those inevitabilities."

You'll find that if you create the goal to become more flexible, some wonderful things will begin to happen: You'll feel more relaxed, yet you won't sacrifice any productivity. You may even become *more* productive because you won't need to expend so much energy being upset and worried. I've learned to trust I will keep my deadlines, achieve most of my goals, and honor my responsibilities despite the fact that I may have to alter my plans slightly (or even completely). Finally, the people around you will be more relaxed too. They won't feel like they have to walk around on eggshells if, by some chance, your plans have to change.

Give Yourself an Extra Ten Minutes

When you ask a typical person or family about what stresses them out the most, it's rare that someone doesn't include the fact that they are almost always running "a few minutes behind." Whether you're off to a soccer match, work, the airport, a neighborhood picnic, a typical day at school, or church, it seems that most of us almost always find a way to wait until the last possible moment to leave, thus running a little late. This tendency creates a great deal of unnecessary stress as we're constantly thinking about who is waiting for us, how far we are behind schedule, and how often this occurs. Invariably, we end up clutching the steering wheel, tightening our neck, and worrying about the consequences of being late. Running late makes us feel stressed out and encourages us to sweat the small stuff!

This ever-so-common problem is easily solved by simply giving yourself an extra ten minutes to get yourself and your family to your appointments. Irrespective of where you're headed, tell yourself that, no matter what, you're going to be ten minutes *early* instead of waiting until the last possible moment to rush out the door.

The key, of course, is to start getting ready a little earlier than usual and to be sure that you're all-the-way ready before you start doing something else. I can't tell you how much this simple strategy has helped me in my own life. Rather than constantly scrambling to find my daughters' shoes or my wallet at the last possible moment, I'm now usually ready with plenty of time to spare. Don't kid yourself that these extra ten minutes aren't significant—they are. The extra few minutes before and between activities can be the difference between a stressful day and a joyful day. In addition, you'll discover that when you're not running late you'll be able to enjoy rather than rush through the different things you do each day. Even simple, ordinary events can be great fun when you're not in such a hurry.

When you're done with one activity, leave a little earlier for the next one. When possible, try to schedule your activities, work, play, and everything else a little further apart. Finally, don't over schedule. Allow for some downtime, time where absolutely nothing is scheduled.

If you implement this strategy, you'll be amazed

at how much more relaxed your life will seem. The constant sense of pressure, of rushing around, scrambling, will be replaced with a quiet sense of peace.

Protect Your Privacy

Your home is your haven, an escape from the outside world. When you allow too much of the craziness from the outside to enter your home, you eliminate, or at least reduce, a potential source of peace. While most of us are concerned with protecting our physical safety, and will take steps to secure it, we often forget or even neglect our emotional and spiritual "safety." We can do this, at least in part, by honoring our need for some degree of privacy.

Protecting and respecting your own privacy is a statement to yourself and others that you value yourself and your own peace of mind. It suggests that your sanity and happiness are extremely important. Your home is one of the few places where, in most instances, you have some degree of control over what enters and what doesn't . Home is often a place where you have the power to say no.

Protecting your privacy can involve many things. It might mean letting your answering machine pick up your messages or screen your calls so that you don't have to. Often, out of pure habit, we rush to pick up the phone when we really don't want to talk to anyone. Is it any wonder we feel overwhelmed or crowded? I have a general policy that I won't answer the phone when I feel like being alone or when I'm already with someone in my family who wants or needs my attention. Why is it that we interrupt the ones we love to answer a call from someone we may not even know?

If you have children, you might try putting a cap on the number of friends you invite to come over in any given week. You do this not to create an anti-social environment but to create a sense of balance and harmony within the home. At various times over the years, my wife and I have felt that our home has seemed more like a train station or a busy bus stop than it has a retreat. By simply acknowledging our desire to create a more peaceful environment and by making a few minor adjustments to protect our privacy, we have been able to bring that balance back into focus.

You can learn to say no more often to requests that would bring you away from home, *and* you can learn to reduce your invitations to friends and others that enter your home. Again, you do this not to become a hermit or alienate your friends and family but to protect and honor your need for privacy.

When you do so, you'll notice a significant difference in the way you feel. You'll feel more nurtured and peaceful. And when you do invite others into your home, and when you accept those gracious invitations from others, you will do so knowing that you are doing so from a place of genuine desire rather than because you feel pressured to do so, out of obligation.

We all need some degree of privacy. When you enter your home, know that it is your own. Whether you rent a small room in someone else's house, occupy an apartment, or own your own home, honor your need for privacy. Before too long, things won't get to you as much.

Don't Answer the Phone

How often have you been completely over-whelmed by all that you're doing at home when, at the worst possible moment, the phone rings? Or, you're trying desperately to get out the door by yourself or with your kids when—*ring, ring ring*—the phone calls out for your attention. Or, on the other end of the spectrum, you're absorbed in a special moment—by yourself or with someone you love—when, again, the phone rings.

The question is, did you answer it? If you're like most people, you probably did. But why? Our response to a ringing phone is one of the few things in life over which we have absolute control and decision-making authority. In this day and age of answering machines and voice mail, it's not as critical to answer the phone as it once was. In most cases, we can simply call someone back at a more convenient time.

In our home, one of the most stressful moments is when the phone rings just as we are going out the door in the morning and one of the kids runs over and answers it! Now, rather than getting in the car, I'm back on the phone addressing someone else's concern. The time and accompanying stress is rarely worth it. I've learned a little secret. I have one of those phones that has a "ringer off" feature. Sometimes, when I remember, I turn the ringer off about thirty minutes before we actually have to leave. This way, the kids won't be tempted to answer the phone.

Many years ago a good friend of mine and I were talking about the issue of answering the phone during a family dinner. We agreed that unless you were expecting a very important call, answering the phone during family time sends a hurtful message to your entire family and is, in fact, disrespectful. The message is: An unknown person is calling and it's more important to me that I answer his or her call than it is to sit with you right now. Pretty scary, isn't it?

Some of my most magical moments with my kids have been when we've been spending time together reading or playing and the phone rings. But rather than interrupting our time together, we look at each other and agree—nothing is more important than our time together right now! This is one of the ways I show my kids how important they are to me. They know I practically live on the phone and my decision to not answer it doesn't come easily.

Obviously, there will be many times when you'll want to answer the phone. I urge you, however, to choose carefully. Ask yourself the question, "Is answering the phone at this moment going to make my life easier, or is it going to add stress to my day?" Simple as it seems, choosing *not* to answer the phone, on selected occasions, can be a very empowering decision and can greatly reduce the stress in your home life.

Live from Your Heart

A subtle yet major contributor to sweating the small stuff for many people is the failure to live from the heart. Instead, many people fall into routines out of default, or because everyone else seems to be doing something, or because it *seems* like the right thing to do. For example, people often choose careers that their parents wanted for them, or because of some perceived status or some other external measure. Or some parents put their kids in certain activities or dress them in a certain way simply because everyone else is doing it. Still others will struggle to buy a home instead of renting an apartment because they heard it was part of the American Dream, or they will, in some other way, live beyond their financial means because they are trying to "keep up with the Joneses."

Living from your heart means that you choose a life and a lifestyle that are true for you and your family. It means you make important decisions because they resonate with your heart and your own values, and not necessarily with those of others. Living from your heart means that you trust your own instincts more than the pressures from advertising or the expectations of society, neighbors, and friends.

Living from your heart, however, does not mean you become a rebel, break family tradition, or become different than everyone else. It's far more subtle than that. Living from the heart is about trusting that quiet voice within you that emerges when you quiet down enough to listen. It's that voice that speaks to you from a place of wisdom and common sense instead of from frantic chatter and habit. When you trust your heart rather than your habits, new insights will pop into your mind. These insights can be anything from the idea to move to a different town, to the realization of the necessity to break a destructive habit, to an answer of how to communicate differently with someone you love. You might also have insights about who you choose to spend your time with as well as new ways to solve problems. It all starts from listening to your heart.

A failure to live from the heart creates a great deal of internal conflict, which in turn encourages you to become short-tempered, easily bothered, and reactive. Deep down, you know what is true for you, what kind of life you want to be living, and what type of person you want to be. If your actions are inconsistent with your deeper wisdom, however, you will feel frustration and stress. As you learn to live from your heart, these tendencies will gradually fade away and you will become calmer, happier, and less stressed. You will be living *your* life instead of everyone else's.

The way to live more from your heart is to commit to doing so. Ask yourself questions like: "How do I really want to live my life?" "Am I following my own path or am I doing things simply because I've always done them that way, or because I'm living up to someone else's expectations?" Then simply quiet down and listen. Rather than trying to come up with an answer, see if you can allow the answers to come to you, as if out of the blue.

16.

Expect It to Spill

I learned this trick more than twenty years ago. It has proven day after day, year after year, to be extremely effective in my goal of creating a more peaceful home environment for myself and for others.

The basis for this strategy stems from the understanding that when we expect something to occur, we are less surprised and therefore less reactive to it. In addition, when we expect something to happen—that is, when we expect something to spill—and it doesn't, we feel grateful. In other words, we begin to appreciate the fact that, a vast majority of the time, the things we are eating and drinking don't get all over the floor and, most of the time, life does go smoothly. The problem is, we tend to focus on the annoying exceptions.

Think back to the last time you or someone in your family spilled a glass of milk or a cup of coffee on the carpet. What was your reaction? In all probability, it involved panic, disappointment, and a great deal of stress. What do you suppose would happen if, instead of assuming that nothing should or will ever spill, you instead expected the beverage to spill—you accept it as inevitable? It puts an entirely different slant on the same set of facts. This doesn't mean you like it when the spill occurs, only that it's okay when it does—you accept it. Obviously, you have no idea when the spill is going to occur, only that, in all likelihood, it will be at some point. It might be later today, next week, or three years from now, but unless you are a rare exception, you will have spilled milk in your home at some point in the future. This strategy prepares you for this inevitable moment.

The same metaphor can easily be extended to virtually any other likely daily annoyance at home—something that doesn't work right, something breaks down, some big mess occurs, someone doesn't do his or her part, whatever! The point is, when you expect something to happen, it won't come as such a surprise when it does. Don't worry that by expecting something to happen you're going to encourage it to take place. You're not. We're not talking about "visualizing" something to happen or encouraging it in any way. We're referring here to the gift of acceptance, learning to accept things as they are instead of pinning our happiness on the way we demand things to be. Watch what happens when you expect something to spill. I'll bet you'll find yourself far more relaxed the next time it occurs.

17

Make Light of Being Overwhelmed

The other day, my wife, Kris, and I broke into one of those belly laughs—the kind where you're laughing so hard that you start to cry. Kris said something to the effect of "This has got to be some sort of divine joke." She was referring to the fact that the two of us had spent several hours picking up the house, putting things away, organizing, and so forth. But, despite our valiant, focused efforts, it was obvious that we were actually moving backward!

No, we're not incompetent. In fact, we're both quite skilled (and practiced) at keeping things clean and neat. The fact was, however, that each of our children had a friend over. One of the kids had tracked mud through our kitchen while Kris was busy cleaning out the closet. (The guilty party had obviously forgotten our "shoes off" policy.) A couple of other kids had been trying to get something out of our daughter's closet when—*bam*—half the toys fell all over the floor. Meanwhile, I was up in the attic attempting to put into boxes some things we were going to give away, when my foot went right through the floor, creating a large hole in the ceiling of the room below. There seemed to be chaos in every room. It was clearly "one of those days." You've undoubtedly had similar experiences at your own home.

At times like these, it's tempting to get really serious and upset. For many of us, there's an almost certain knee-jerk reaction of telling yourself how unfair life is and convincing yourself how useless your efforts are. Frequently, during stressful and frustrating times like these, we mentally review how many times this has happened in the past and how likely it is to occur in the future. Needless to say, however, none of this mental rehearsal does the least bit of good.

One of the more effective ways of dealing with being overwhelmed is to step back from the situation and see the humor. As Kris pointed out, "If someone were secretly watching this scene, they would be in hysterics, laughing at us!" It was at that point that we both lightened up about the whole scenario.

Does this mean we didn't care about the mess? Absolutely not. If anything, Kris and I are neat freaks. Both of us prefer and love a clean, orderly home. There are times, however, when you simply don't have control over your environment—especially if you have one or more children. Sometimes there are too many people in your living space, or too many things going on, or not enough time, or whatever. This isn't to suggest you shouldn't try, only to remind you that you're only human. There is just so much a person can do.

When you attempt to see the humor in your fruitless efforts, it takes the pressure off feeling as though you have to be perfect, or that you have to maintain a perfect house. Instead of scrambling out of frustration to "get it all done," you might be able to come to peace with the fact that, even if you dust the last table, it will probably be dusty again in a day or so. Humor doesn't keep your house clean or organized, but it does give you perspective and make you feel better. Without minimizing its importance, it does remind you not to take your chores and responsibilities so seriously.

18

Refuse to Let It Bug You

This is a fun one to practice if you have kids, but undoubtedly as effective if you do not. Refusing to "let it bug you" can apply to virtually anything—kids' fighting or demanding your attention, chaos, a messy room, a leaking roof, a noisy pet, an overflowing closet, or a snoring spouse.

Not all, but certainly part, of the problem with overreactivity stems from our habitual reactions to events that are largely beyond our control. For example, when the kids are fighting and it feels like it's going to drive you crazy, your knee-jerk reaction might be to get angry and send the kids to their rooms. Then you compound the problem by thinking to yourself, "I can't believe how often this happens," or "I can't believe how difficult it is to raise kids," or some other equally validating statement designed to convince you that you couldn't possibly respond in any other way! In our own minds, we blow the issue out of proportion by overanalyzing and discussing it with others. Pretty soon, this and other "small stuff" starts to seem like really big stuff.

It's entirely possible to train your mind to be less reactive to ordinarily difficult events. When you refuse to let it bug you, you are not denying that something bugs you. What you *are* doing is retraining your mind to respond differently to the same set of facts. You begin by telling yourself, in advance of a normally difficult scenario, "I will not be bothered by, or overreact to, this event."

On the surface, and in the beginning, this may

seem a little superficial. After all, telling yourself you're not going to be bothered can seem a little like telling yourself you feel good when you are experiencing the flu! However, if you give it a chance, I think you'll find this strategy surprisingly effective. Be patient and give it some time. If you anticipate your own responses to life, it takes the habitual reactivity out of the picture. You will know, in advance, what your response is going to be, and you are merely using your life circumstances to practice those responses. In this way, you turn what might normally seem like a burden into an inner game.

I can't tell you how effective this has been with my own two children. Like most people, I've over-reacted many times with each of my children. When I use this strategy, however, it seems to break most negative patterns that we develop through habit. Just the other day, the kids got into one of their squabbles, yelling and blaming each other. I could see it coming and silently told myself, "I refuse to be bothered by this upcoming fight." The result was one of those rare moments every parent longs for—stunned children! I sat casually on the couch, not lifting my head from my book, even for a moment. Within two minutes, the kids were absolutely silent, wondering what was wrong with me. Their dispute magically disappeared without any involvement on my part. We ended up enjoying the rest of the afternoon. You'll have fun with this one.

19

Experience Calm Surrender

Calm surrender is a term I use to describe the process of "letting go" around the home and elsewhere. Simply put, it means surrendering with grace and humility, to the chaos of life. It's a form of acceptance, of being okay with what is, of ending the struggle.

Often, we struggle against aspects of life that are largely beyond our control—noise, confusion, comments we don't approve of, lost items, rudeness, imperfections, negativity, broken pipes, clogged drains, whatever. We fight, get angry and annoyed, and wish things were different. We complain, fret, and commiserate. Yet, when you add up all this frustration, the end result is always the same: The things we are frustrated about remain as they are. No amount of gritting our teeth or clenching our fists makes the least bit of difference. In fact, it only adds fuel to the fire, often making things worse than they already are.

Calm surrender is not about giving up. Nor is it about being apathetic, lazy, or not caring. Instead, it's about appropriate acceptance, being willing to let go of our insistence that the events in our lives be any certain way or different than they actually are. The wisdom of this strategy is simple: Although you might wish things were different (or demand it), they are not. They are exactly as they are. This doesn't mean you shouldn't make changes or encourage improvements—you absolutely should do so in those instances where you feel it's important or necessary.

What this strategy is addressing is the frustration that comes from not having things go your way.

The way to experience calm surrender is to start with little things. For example, while doing the dishes, you prove your humanness and drop and break a plate. Rather than yell and scream and stomp your feet, see if you can accept the moment for what it is— a moment that includes a broken dish. No big deal, no need for fret, no need to panic. Just loving acceptance for the truth of the moment. There before you, on the ground, is a broken plate. The question is: What are you going to do now? The plate is already broken. You can tense your arms and perhaps break another plate, or you can relax and see the humor in the fact that we are all so imperfect. Another example might be an interaction with your spouse. If he or she says something that might usually annoy you, see if you can respond a little differently. Instead of being bothered by your spouse's need to criticize, for example, see if you can "brush if off," love him or her in spite of the comment. Again, the comment has already been made. Your reaction to that comment is up to you. If you can change your habitual reactions to include more peaceful responses, you'll quickly see that everything will be all right, it's all okay.

In our home we have a little saying that one of the kids made up. I've always thought it's a great way to describe calm surrender. When something breaks or something really goes wrong, one of the kids will say, "Oh, well, everything happens!" in other words, what's the use of struggling?

This strategy is particularly effective when there is great chaos going on around the home. Yesterday, I was home with both kids and two of their friends. All the kids were hungry, and I hadn't cleaned up the last mess. The phone rang at the same moment the doorbell did. For a moment, I thought I was going to go nuts, and then I remembered to take a deep breath and let go. In that moment of chaos, the best I could do was experience calm surrender, to simply relax. And the interesting thing to me was that in this, as well as in every other instance like it that I can remember, the moment I relaxed and stopped struggling, everything began to calm down.

If you are willing to give this strategy a try, you'll be amazed at the results. The calmer you become, the easier your life will be. Rather than exacerbating negative events and bringing out the worst in other people, you'll begin to stop negativity before it has a chance to spiral any further. In time, and with a little practice, you'll begin to experience chaos in a whole new light. There will be so much less drama in your life. So, starting today, see if you can ease the chaos by experiencing calm surrender.

20.

Create a "Selfish" Ritual

It has always amused me when people have responded to my suggestion that they take care of their own needs with the question, "Wouldn't that be selfish?" I'd like to take this opportunity to put that concern to rest! This strategy stems from the understanding that when you have what you need, in an emotional sense, you have plenty left over for other people and their needs.

If your goal is to become more relaxed and happy at home, one of the most helpful things you can do is to create an activity that is yours exclusively, something you do—just for you. For example, my private ritual is to get up really early in the morning before anyone else in my family. I use this time to stretch, have a quiet cup of coffee, and read a chapter or two in my favorite book. Sometimes I meditate or reflect on my life. I cherish this special ritual in my day.

Obviously, everyone is different. Some people like to squeeze a little exercise into their routine—creating a healthy ritual. Others like to browse bookstores or have a quiet cup of coffee before work. Still others like to take a warm bath or shower at a predetermined time. The point is, it's your time—a special part of the day that is reserved for you.

A ritual that I used to practice, that I've shared with many others, is that I would stop a few blocks from my home on my way home from work. I'd pull off the road in an area where there were lots of trees and plants. And for just a few minutes, I'd simply look at the beauty around me. Nothing fancy, not too much time. But just enough to give me a breather between my work life and coming home to energetic kids who wanted and deserved my attention. During those few minutes, I'd breathe deeply and remind myself how lucky I was to be going home to a loving family. I'd look in awe at the beautiful trees and plants. Then, after a few minutes, I'd start the car and drive home.

The difference in how I felt when I took this time was enormous. Rather than rushing to the door tired and grumpy, I'd feel relaxed and loving. I could tell the difference in my reception from my family as well. Apparently, they could sense my peace.

Whether you get up a little earlier, take a regular bath, or stop and smell the roses on your way home from work, do something. Create a ritual that is just for you. You'll be amazed at how much value you get out of so few minutes.

21

If You Have Children, Set Your Agenda Aside

Admittedly, this is a tough strategy to implement. Yet, if you give it a try, I think you'll see it's worth the effort. In case you haven't noticed, when you have no agenda at home (or at least less agenda), you'll usually have a better day than when you have a fixed plan that you're determined to stick to. When you are emotionally and rigidly tied to your plan, you'll almost always end up disappointed, as though you didn't complete enough items on your list. And even if you do, you'll be exhausted and perhaps resentful at how difficult it was to get it all done.

Obviously, there are times you must have an agenda and a plan, and at other times you'll have tasks you must complete and goals to attend to. But the spirit of this suggestion is what's most helpful. Try to see how your own rigidity, your mental ties to your plan, tend to stress you out. And not only that—you may discover that the more attached to your agenda you are, the less you actually get done. This is due to the fact that a rigid attitude makes it awkward, if not impossible, to shift gears and to go with the flow. When you have children to care for, it's almost impossible to know exactly what is going to occur on any given day. To flow with the changes and uncertainties requires an ability to be flexible and responsive.

Often, a wise idea is to keep your agenda on your back burner. In other words, know what it is you would *ideally* like to accomplish but let go of your attachment to getting it done. Then, when possible, gently seize the opportunities you have to work toward those goals. For example, you might have the goal of returning three phone calls, getting your car in for repair, and getting the grocery shopping done. Rather than being frustrated by the fact that you haven't had a moment to yourself to achieve any of these goals, be as patient as you possibly can be. Relax. Don't fill your mind with additional verification that you're "trapped at home" or that you're overwhelmed. Instead, keep your attention in the present moment as best you can. If you stay calm and responsive rather than agitated and hurried, you'll sense when the opportunity arises to attend to your agenda. Because you are in a responsive state of mind, you'll take advantage of any opportunities that present themselves and attend to your responsibilities in a wise and timely manner.

And even if you never do get the opportunities you had hoped for on any given day, you'll be able to keep your perspective and remember, in the long run, that this will all be seen as "small stuff."

22

Keep a Sane Pace

Today, more than ever, many of us live at a pace that can only be described as "crazy." In addition to the incredible demands of simply getting by, earning a living, raising a family, and attending to our daily responsibilities, many of us also attempt to partake in social, fitness, charitable or volunteer, and recreational activities as well. We are trying desperately to stay fit and be good parents, citizens, and friends. If at all possible, most of us would also like to have some fun. The problem is, each of us has only twenty-four hours in a day. There is only so much we can do.

There are many contributing factors to this

increased pace of life, including technology and higher expectations. Computers, electronics, and other forms of technology have made our world seem smaller and masked our limitation of time. We can do everything much more quickly than ever before. Unfortunately, this has contributed to a sense of impatience, of wanting things to happen immediately. I've seen people annoyed because they had to wait a few minutes at a fast-food restaurant, or bothered because their computers took more than a few seconds to boot up. We get stressed over a little traffic and completely lose sight of the fact that we're traveling relatively quickly in a comfortable automobile or bus. Indeed, it seems that our expectations have increased to the point that many of us want to do everything. Nothing is good enough—we have to have more and do more.

If we try to do too much, we end up frantically

rushing around from one thing to the next. And when we are hurried, we are more easily bothered and have the tendency to sweat the small stuff! In addition, when we are rushed, we rarely feel a sense of satisfaction for what we are doing because we are so focused on getting to the next activity. Instead of being in the moment, we are off to the next one.

Keeping a sane pace does more than keep us sane. It brings a richness to our experience that is impossible to experience when we are rushing around too quickly. There is something magical about having a little space between activities, a sense of calm, of having enough time. I have found that keeping a sane pace is a reward in and of itself, a satisfying experience in its own right.

If I had to choose between doing five things in a hurried, rushed manner, or four things calmly and peacefully, I'd choose the latter. Obviously, there will be times when rushing around is a fact of life that you may not be able to avoid. Sometimes, it seems that you have to be in two or three places at the same time! However, there is usually some amount of rushing around that is self-created. By simply becoming aware of your own speeded-up tendency, and by having the goal of keeping a sane pace, you may find subtle ways to slow down your life and become a little calmer and stress free. I think you'll find that if you can slow down, even slightly, the quality of your life will be enhanced in many ways.

23.

Don't Be a Martyr

Needless to say, we all make sacrifices and trade-offs in our relationships and family lives. Most of these sacrifices are well worth it. But, as with most things (including good things), too much is still too much.

Obviously, the tolerance levels to stress, responsibility, lack of sleep, sacrifice, hardship, and everything else are going to vary from person to person. In other words, something that's supereasy for you can be quite difficult for me—and vice versa. However, if we can pay attention to, and be honest about, our feelings, each of us knows when the level of stress has risen too high. When it does, we usually feel incredibly frustrated, agitated, and perhaps most of all, resentful. We may feel a little self-righteous and convince ourselves that we're working harder than other people and that we have it tougher than anyone else.

Many of us (myself included) have fallen prey to the seduction of becoming a martyr. It's easy to have this happen because there is often a fine line between working hard out of actual necessity and overdoing it out of perceived necessity.

The sad truth is, however, that no one actually benefits from or appreciates a martyr. To himself, a martyr is his own worst enemy—constantly filling his head with lists of things to do and always reminding himself how difficult his life is. This mental ambush saps the joy from his life. And to the people around him, a martyr is an overly serious complainer who is too self-absorbed to see the beauty of life. Rather than feeling sorry for him, or seeing him as a victim, as the martyr would love to see happen, outsiders usually see the martyr's problems as completely self-created.

If you think you may have martyr tendencies, I urge you to give them up! Rather than spending 100 percent of your energy doing things for other people, leave something for someone else to do. Take up a hobby. Spend a few minutes a day doing something just for you—something you really enjoy. You'll be amazed by two things. First, you'll actually start to enjoy your life and experience more energy as you feel less stressed. Nothing takes more energy than feeling resentful and victimized. Second, as you let go of resentment and the feeling that everything you do is out of obligation, the others around you will begin to appreciate you more than before. Rather than feeling as if you resent them, they will feel as if you enjoy and appreciate them instead—which you will. In short, everyone wins and benefits when you give up your victim attitude and your tendency to be a martyr.

24

Let Go of Your Expectations

If ever there was a suggestion that was easier said than done, this would be it. Expectations are part of life and seem to be ingrained into our thinking. However, if you can lessen your expectations (even a little bit) about how things are supposed to be, and instead open your heart and accept what is, you'll be well on your way to a calmer and much happier life.

The truth is, our expectations are responsible for a great deal of grief and stress. We expect something to be a certain way or a person to behave in a certain way and it doesn't happen—so we get upset, bothered, disappointed, and unhappy. Since life is rarely exactly the way we would like it to be, or the way we expect it to be, we end up spending a great deal of time let down or disappointed, constantly wishing life were different than it actually is. Then, rather than seeing our own part in the process, we continue to blame life and our circumstances for our stress and frustration.

Just yesterday, Kris caught me in this psychological trap. I tend to be a very enthusiastic person, and one of my buttons is when other people (especially my family) fail to meet my expectation that they should also be enthusiastic. In this particular instance, it was a really hot day and I was excited about going to the community pool where we are members. But when I asked the kids if they wanted to go along with me, their response was less than I had hoped for. Instead of "Great idea, Dad, we can't wait," it was a little more like "Yeah, whatever." Their response sent me into a tailspin as I blurted out the question, "What's wrong with everyone around here?" It probably would have gotten worse, but Kris jumped in and with a smile said, "What was it that you were saying about opening your heart to 'what is' instead of insisting on it being a certain way?" Enough said!

In no way am I suggesting that you eliminate your preferences or all of your expectations. Certainly there will be times when you will want to insist on certain things or demand certain standards of behavior, and that's fine. But lessening your expectations is *not* the same thing as lowering your standards! It's entirely possible to have very high standards, yet still keep your perspective about your own expectations. Keep in mind that our goal here is to improve the quality of our lives and to keep the little things from taking over our lives. It's ultimately in your best interest if you can see the importance of letting go of some of your expectations. That way, you can enjoy more of your life the way it really is and struggle less with the way you would rather it be.

25

Appreciate Your In-laws

Admittedly, this has been an easy one for me because my in-laws, Pat and Ted, are extraordinary people. And I must say that my wife is equally lucky because my parents are also quite special. However, for most people, in-laws present quite a personal challenge, to say the least. And even if you do like your in-laws, you do have to make certain sacrifices simply because of the nature of marriage. You will, for example, have to make trade-offs as to where you spend holidays. You will also have to deal with the most unavoidable problems of conflicting backgrounds and upbringings—different religious philosophies, differing views on parenting, discipline, spending, saving, the relative importance of spending time with family, and so forth. Yet, despite probable differences among you, I believe that most in-law relationships have the potential to be loving and filled with mutual respect.

The trick to making the most of your relationship with you in-laws is to stay focused on gratitude. While there almost certainly will be differences you will have to deal with, gratitude will enable you to appreciate, rather than struggle against, those differences.

It's easy to forget, yet of you love your spouse, you owe your in-laws and enormous debt of gratitude! If not for their bringing your spouse into the world, you would be with someone else, or alone. In most instances, it took your in-laws (or one of them) to raise your spouse. So, regardless of what you may think, they played a significant role in your spouse's upbringing.

Before you sarcastically think something like, "That explains why my spouse has certain problems," keep in mind that the opposite is equally true. If you blame your in-laws for any issues your spouse struggles with, it's only fair to give them credit for his or her strengths as well. In addition, if you have children, their genes—their physical makeup—come, in part, from your in-laws. Without their contribution, your children would not be the people they are. If you think your kids are cute, and who doesn't think so, some of that cuteness, whether you want to believe it or not, comes from your in-laws.

Believe me, I'm not a bury-your-head-in-the-sand-and pretend-everything-is-perfect kind of person. I realize that all in-laws have certain difficult qualities, just as I will to my future son-in-law, someday down the road (way down the road). However, what choice do you have? You can continue to complain about your in-laws, make mean-spirited jokes about how difficult it is to have them, and wish that they were different—or you can begin to focus less on their irritating quirks and characteristics and instead focus on that which you have to be grateful for. I believe the decision is an easy one. Stay focused on gratitude and my guess is that you'll be able to improve your existing relationship in a significant way.

26

Don't Sweat the Little Quirks

In some ways, it's no wonder that the people you live with can drive you crazy with their little quirks. You know, the way someone eats, uses utensils, breathes, flits her hair, jiggles his leg, stacks pennies, or stomps his or her feet, or whatever. After all, chances are you spend more time with these people than anyone else. Therefore, you have far more opportunities to experience and become familiar with the quirks and idiosyncrasies of your family than you do with anyone else. Over time, you come to expect, even anticipate, these quirks, and when they occur they tend to annoy you.

Let's face it. There isn't a person alive who doesn't have his or her share of irritating quirks. I have so many I'd be embarrassed to share them with you. And if you were really honest, I'll bet you'd admit to having a few of your own. But despite these innocent quirks, I'll bet you're a really nice person with many fine qualities. I'd like to think I fall into the same category.

The point is, we're all human. Whether you live alone and only have to deal with your own little quirks (or those of any pets you might have), or whether you have a spouse and a bunch of kids and have dozens of quirks to contend with on a regular basis, we're all in this together. To be human is to have quirks. Big deal!

Many people are easily bothered by their own quirks and by those of their family members. They focus on them and wish they would go away. They share their displeasure with their closest friends. But guess what? The chances of those pesky quirks going away are about as good as my chances of winning the Wimbledon tennis championship—zero, none. Okay, maybe once in a great while someone will outgrow an annoying quirk and/or change a pattern or habit. But this is extremely rare and, in most cases, highly unlikely. Think about it. Doesn't the friend in whom you're confiding regarding your spouse's irritating quirks have a few of his or her own? What's more, do you think your friend might, on occasion, discuss your little imperfections with his or her other friends?

You really only have two options when it comes to quirks. You can continue to be critical of, and be bothered by, the little quirks that exist in your household. Or you can choose to see the innocence and humor that is inherent in virtually all quirks. After all, no one wants annoying quirks to be part of his or her personal makeup—we certainly don't set out to create them! They develop unintentionally and continue out of pure habit. In addition, it's important to keep in mind that, if you were to live with someone else, he or she too would quickly exhibit a variety of quirks. And who knows? They might be even more annoying than the ones you are currently forced to deal with.

Why not make the decision to make those little quirks a little less relevant? Doing so is a huge relief. You will no longer have to spend mental energy reminding yourself how irritated you are—therefore feeling the effects of that irritation. And you'll find that when you're more forgiving and accepting of everyone else, it's far easier to be easier on yourself. So, starting today, whatever "small stuff" around the house bugs you, see if you can let it go! You'll be so much happier as a result.

27

When Someone Asks You How You Are, Don't Emphasize How Busy You Are

Putting too much emphasis on our busyness has become a way of life, almost a knee-jerk reaction. In fact, I'd guess that one of the most common responses to the greeting "How are you doing?" has become "I'm so busy." As I write about this strategy, I have to admit that, at times, I'm as guilty of this tendency as anyone else. However, I've noticed that as I become more conscious of it, I'm putting less and less emphasis on my busyness—and I'm feeling a whole lot better as a result.

It's almost as though we become more comfortable after confirming to others that, we too, are very busy. I was in the grocery store last night on my way home from work when I witnessed two sets of friends greeting one another. The first person said, "Hi, Chuck. How's it going?" Chuck sighed loudly and said, "Really busy, how about you?" His friend responded, "Yeah, me too. I've been working really hard."

Then, almost as if the customers in the store knew I was writing a book, two women added to my material! Not more than a few seconds later, out of the corner of my eye, I heard one woman say to the other, "Grace, nice to see you. How's everything?" Grace's response was to noticeably shrug her shoulders and say, "Pretty good, but really busy," followed by a polite and seemingly sincere "How about you?" the answer: "You know, busy as ever."

It's very tempting to enter into a conversation

with these words because the truth is that most of us are really busy. Also, many people feel they have to be busy or they have no value in our society. Some people are even competitive about how busy they are. The problem, however, is that this response and overemphasis on how busy we are sets the tone for the rest of the conversation. It puts the emphasis on busyness by reminding both parties how stressful and complicated life has become. So, despite the fact that you have a moment to escape your stressful existence by saying hello to a friend or acquaintance, you are choosing to spend even your spare moments emphasizing and reminding yourself how busy you are.

Despite the fact that this response may have elements of honesty, it works against you—and your friend—by reinforcing your feelings of busyness. True, you're busy, but that's not all you are! You're also an interesting person with many other qualities besides busyness. The fact that most of us emphasize how busy we are to others isn't entirely necessary but is simply a habit many of us have fallen into. We can change this habit by simply recognizing that it exists—and exploring other options.

I think you'll be amazed at how much more relaxed you'll become if you do nothing more than change your initial comments to people you see or talk to on the phone. As an experiment, try to eliminate any discussion about how busy you are for an entire week! It may be difficult, but it will be worth it. You'll notice that, despite being as busy as ever, you'll begin to feel slightly less busy. You'll also notice that, as you deemphasize how busy you are, the people you speak with will sense permission from you to place a little less emphasis on their own busyness, helping them feel a little less stressed and perhaps encouraging your entire conversation to be more nourishing and jointly relaxing. So, the next time someone asks you how you are doing, say anything except "I'm really busy." You'll be glad you did.

28.

Treat Your Family Members as if This Were the Last Time You Were Going to See Them

It's always difficult to know how to end a book. In *Don't Sweat the Small Stuff*, I concluded by suggesting that you live as if today were your last day on earth—because it might be; you never really know. I decided to bring this book to its conclusion by making a similar suggestion, only this time geared toward your family. In this strategy, I suggest that you treat your family members (and those you love most) as if this were the last time you were going to see them.

How often do we run out the door without saying good-bye—or say something less than kind or something critical under our breath as a parting shot as we go our separate ways? How often do we take for granted those we love and count on the most, assuming we will *always* be together? Most of us seem to operate under the assumption that we can always be kind later, that there's always tomorrow. But is that a wise way to live?

A few years ago, my grandmother Emily passed away. I remember visiting her, knowing that each visit might very well be the last time I ever saw her. Each visit counted and was treated special. Each good-bye was filled with a genuine love, appreciation, and reflection. Looking back, it was a particularly loving time because each moment was precious.

Our daily lives can be this precious. A powerful exercise to practice on a regular basis is to imagine that this is your final good-bye. Imagine that, for one reason or another, you won't see your family member ever again after this meeting. If this were true (and it's always a possibility), would you think and act in the same way? Would you remind your parent, child, sibling, spouse, or other loved one of yet another shortcoming, flaw, or imperfection in his or her behavior or personality? Would your last words be complaints or pessimistic comments that suggest you wish your life were different than it is?

Probably not.

Perhaps, if you thought there was always the possibility that this were the last time you were going to see someone you love, you'd take an extra minute to give a loving hug and say good-bye. Or maybe you'd say something kind and gentle, an affirmation of your love, instead of your business-as-usual "See you later." If you thought this were the last time you were going to see your teenager, sister, parent, in-law, or spouse, you might treat that person differently, with more kindness, and more compassionately. Rather than rushing away, you'd probably smile and tell the person how much you care. Your heart would be open.

I make this suggestion not to create a fearful environment but to encourage you to remember how precious your family is and how much you'd miss them if they (or you) weren't around to share your life with you. The implementation of this strategy into my life has added additional perspective to what's most important. I believe it can help you to become more patient and loving—and perhaps most of all, to remember to not sweat the small stuff with your family.